To Sheenal

May the Lo[rd] ... om
as yo...

Pearls of

For That Notorious First Year & Forever After

— *For Her* —

Mothers like to give advice to their daughters when they leave their parents house. Today 25.5.08 I give you this book so that when you read it God will advice you in every di[lemma] of your life. Love Mum xxx

Pearls of Wisdom

For That Notorious First Year & Forever After

— *For Her* —

Clara Hinton

New Leaf Press

First Edition
September 1994

Copyright © 1994 by Clara Hinton. All rights reserved. Printed in the United States of America. No part of this book may be used or reproduced in any manner whatsoever without written permission of the publisher, except in the case of brief quotations in articles and reviews. For information write: New Leaf Press, Inc., P.O. Box 311, Green Forest, AR 72638.

ISBN: 0-89221-272-1

Unless noted otherwise, Bible Scripture is from the New American Standard Version. JBP denotes the J.B. Phillips translation, NCV denotes the New Century Version, and NIV denotes the New International Version.

*This book is dedicated with all of Mom's love to
Michelle and Eric, Mike and Ashley, Dave and Cynthia,
and all of my treasures who will one day go through that
"Notorious First Year."*

Introduction

If marriage is such a wonderful thing, then why do so many give up early in the game and look for a way out? That first year seems to be an incredibly difficult one for most couples. We go into this union so in love, blind to everything and everyone about us. And then it happens. Problems begin creeping into the relationship, and we don't know what is wrong. The whole thing seems like one big failure. This can't be what married life is all about! Adjustments. Attitudes. Bills. Responsibilities. Moods. Sharing. Boredom. Homesickness. Feeling abandoned at times. Where is this wedded bliss?

I, like so many others, went through a very difficult first year of marriage with my husband. Many doors were slammed, buckets of tears were shed, and there were many days of hardly speaking. Trying. Failing. Trying again. Wanting things to be different, but not knowing quite what to do.

Some 24 years and 11 children later, married life has not only survived, but has even managed to flourish! But it has not been easy. There have been compromises, adjustments, and much forgiveness all along the way.

Something still amazes me, though. When problems crop up (yes, they still do!), many of them relate back in some way to the very problems we experienced during that "notorious first year." Not long ago, this really hit home. My husband had to work out of town for a day and didn't know when he would return home that evening. As always, I reminded him to call me when he knew what his schedule would be. I simply wanted to know when I might expect him. At five minutes after twelve midnight, I received a phone call.

"Honey, I've been in Philadelphia and have several hours of driving yet to do. I'll see you in the morning." I could feel the blood warming in my veins! After these many years of marriage, it was amazing to me that my husband could still innocently "forget" to call home. He just got busy, had several appointments, and forgot.

The outcome of that episode is this book. I believe with all of my heart that most of us get lazy very early on in our married relationship. On top of that, very few of us know how to properly communicate with our mate. We need constant reminders and guidelines to help us get back on track, and to stay on track, whether it's that "fickle first year" or that "flourishing fiftieth year."

This book is an outpouring of love and wisdom accumulated over many years of trial and error, laughter and tears, and learning and re-learning. These "pearls" are meant to stimulate, challenge, encourage, and motivate us in our married lives. It is my sincere prayer that these "pearls" will help every married couple arrive back at the point where they began — with a pure, innocent, blinding love for one another, but equipped with the wisdom to keep this union of love bound, forevermore.

                              Lovingly,
                              Clara Hinton

Learn to communicate;
it takes lots of time.

"Words from the mouth of a wise man are gracious, while the lips of a fool consume him" (Eccles. 10:12).

Forgive quickly.

"But if you do not forgive, neither will your Father who is in heaven forgive your transgressions" (Mark 11:26).

Be your husband's best friend.

"A friend loves at all times" (Prov. 17:17).

Give your husband your heart.

"It is hard to find a good wife, because she is worth more than rubies. Her husband trusts her completely. With her, he has everything he needs. She does him good and not harm for as long as she lives" (Prov. 31:10-12).

Men think differently than women. Learn that fact early on.

"Then the Lord God said, 'It is not good for the man to be alone. I will make a helper who is right for him' "
(Gen. 2:18;NCV).

Fix one special meal a week just for him.

"She rises also while it is still night and gives food to her household" (Prov. 31:15).

When you quarrel, don't call home to mother. Mothers have long memories and active tongues.

"Don't always go to your family for help when trouble comes" (Prov. 27:10;NCV).

Neatness is not as important to most men as women, so relax in this area some.

"Encourage the young women to love their husbands, to love their children, to be sensible, pure, workers at home, kind, being subject to their own husbands, that the word of God may not be dishonored" (Titus 2:4-5).

Buy him a calendar and mark all special dates on it in **bold** lettering.

"There is an appointed time for everything. And there is a time for every event under heaven" (Eccles. 11:8;NCV).

Expect immaturity for a while. It takes time to grow up.

"When I was a child, I used to speak as a child, think as a child, reason as a child; when I became a man, I did away with childish things" (1 Cor. 13:11).

Don't make him your entire life; that puts a drain on a marriage.

"Have you found honey? Eat only what you need"
(Prov. 25:16).

Don't expect the honeymoon to last forever.

"In the day of prosperity be happy, but in the day of adversity consider — God has made the one as well as the other so that man may not discover anything that will be after him" (Eccles. 7:14).

Learn real fast to overlook a lot.

"Indeed, there is not a righteous man on earth who continually does good and who never sins"
(Eccles. 7:20)

Gentle words generally get the job done quicker than harsh words.

"A gentle answer turns away wrath, but a harsh word stirs up anger" (Prov. 15:1).

Bickering is inevitable; try to end a bicker in its early stages before it becomes a fight.

"Starting a quarrel is like a leak in a dam, so stop it before a fight breaks out" (Prov. 17:14;NCV).

Never laugh at your husband's dreams.

"What you say can mean life or death. Those who speak with care will be rewarded" (Prov. 18:21;NCV).

Teach your husband the art of cuddling.

". . . put on love, which is the perfect bond of unity"
(Col. 3:14).

Hold hands often.

". . . I held on to him and would not let him go"
(Song of Sol. 3:4).

Argue a point, not the person.

"Cease from anger and forsake wrath; do not fret, it leads only to evil doing" (Ps. 37:8).

Learn to share.

"And do not neglect doing good and sharing; for with such sacrifices God is pleased" (Heb. 13:16).

Plan outings together.

"A plan in the heart of a man is like deep water"
(Prov. 20:5).

Don't put him down. And **never** put him down in front of someone.

"An excellent wife is the crown of her husband, but she who shames him is as rottonness in his bones"
(Prov. 12:4).

Learn to keep private talk private.

"As a ring of gold in a swine's snout, so is a beautiful woman who lacks discretion" (Prov. 11:22).

Talk before going to bed.

"Worry is a heavy load, but a kind word cheers you up"
(Prov. 12:25;NCV).

Do not worry about problems that do not have an immediate solution.

"And which of you by being anxious can add a single cubit to his life's span?" (Matt. 6:27).

Give your husband some time alone each week.

"And after He had sent the multitudes away, He went up to the mountain by Himself to pray; and when it was evening, He was there alone" (Matt. 14:23).

Don't try to be perfect; that will never happen.

"Indeed, there is not a righteous man on earth who continually does good and who never sins"
(Eccles. 7:20).

Think before you speak.

"He who guards his mouth and his tongue guards his soul from trouble" (Prov. 21:23).

Crying the first year is normal. You are making major adjustments every day.

"I am weary with my sighing; every night I make my bed swim, I dissolve my couch with tears" (Ps. 6:6).

Don't expect too much in bed. It takes time and practice to learn from each other.

"Let the husband fulfill his duty to his wife, and likewise also the wife to her husband" (1 Cor. 7:3).

Don't involve others in your upsets. Try to work small problems out yourselves.

"Do not forsake your own friend or your father's friend, and do not go to your brother's house in the day of your calamity" (Prov. 27:10).

Pretend you are still dating. He will seem more exciting.

"Among the young men, my lover is like an apple tree in the woods! I enjoy sitting in his shadow; his fruit is sweet to my taste" (Song of Sol. 2:3;NCV).

Allow room for some doubts. It's all part of the first year.

"Don't be too right, and don't be too wise. Why destroy yourself?" (Eccles. 7:16;NCV).

Focus on his good points and diminish the bad.

"And why do you look at the speck that is in your brother's eye, but do not notice the log that is in your own eye?" (Matt. 7:3).

Remember how happy you felt with this man before you were married?

"You are so handsome, my lover, and so pleasant!"
(Song of Sol. 1:16;NCV).

Plan time with other couples. It is healthy to laugh and be with others your own age.

"Young people, enjoy yourselves while you are young; be happy while you are young" (Eccles. 11:9;NCV).

Laugh often.

"A joyful heart is good medicine, but a broken spirit dries up the bones" (Prov. 17:22).

Get away from the house or apartment together. Home seems great after some time away.

"Come, my beloved, let us go out into the country, let us spend the night in the villages" (Song of Sol. 7:11).

Don't expect every luxury in life all at once.

"And if we have food and covering, with these we shall be content" (1 Tim. 6:8).

Be happy and make the most of what you have.

"Let your character be free from the love of money, being content with what you have" (Heb. 13:5).

Tell him you appreciate his hard work.

"Let him . . . labor, performing with his own hands what is good, in order that he may have something to share with him that has need" (Eph. 4:28).

Look for the rainbows; don't always point out the clouds.

"Those who wait for perfect weather will never plant seeds; those who look at every cloud will never harvest crops" (Eccles. 11:4;NCV).

Hold each other close at least once a day.

"Let his left hand be under my head and his right hand embrace me" (Song of Sol. 8:3).

Say **"I love you"** at least once a day, even when you are upset.

"Love never ends" (1 Cor. 13:8;NCV).

Live today, but dream of the future together.

"It is sad not to get what you hoped for. But wishes that come true are like eating fruit from the tree of life" (Prov. 13:12;NCV).

Share setting the budget, paying the bills, and managing the finances.

"The wise woman builds her house, but the foolish tears it down with her own hands" (Prov. 14:1).

Know that **it will get better.**

"Many are the afflictions of the righteous; but the Lord delivers him out of them all" (Ps. 34:19).

Learn to say "I'm sorry."

*"He who conceals his transgression will not prosper,
but he who confesses and forsakes them
will find compassion"* (Prov. 28:13).

Don't bring up previous boyfriends.

"But refuse foolish and ignorant speculations, knowing that they produce quarrels" (2 Tim. 2:23).

Give a relaxing back rub. It can work wonders.

"Generous people will be blessed" (Prov. 22:9;NCV).

Never make a major decision alone.

"Without consultation, plans are frustrated, but with many counselors they succeed" (Prov. 15:22).

Tuck a love note in your husband's lunch.

*"When you talk, do not say harmful things,
but say what people need — words that will help others
become stronger. Then what you say will do good
to those who listen to you"* (Eph. 4:29;NCF).

Compliment your husband to others.

"My husband is dazzling and ruddy, outstanding among ten thousand" (Song of Sol. 5:10).

Never make fun of your husband's insecurities.

"The devising of folly is sin, and the scoffer is an abomination to men" (Prov. 24:9).

Serve your husband breakfast in bed occasionally.

"She rises while it is still night, and gives food to her household" (Prov. 31:15).

Keep yourself looking neat and clean. Use his favorite perfume.

"Wash yourself, put on perfume, change your clothes"
(Ruth 3:3;NCV).

Tell your husband what is bothering you. Don't make him play the guessing game.

"Spoken words can be like deep water . . . wisdom is like a flowing stream" (Prov. 18:4;NCV).

Ask. Don't give orders like a drill sergeant.

". . . Ask what you wish me to give you" (1 Kings 3:5).

Be innovative with your finances. Learn to stretch a little to go a long way.

"I know how to get along with humble means, and I also know how to live in prosperity; in any and every circumstance I have learned the secret of being filled and going hungry, both of having abundance and suffering need" (Phil. 4:12).

Relax — most problems are not life threatening.

"The smart person says very little, and one with understanding stays calm" (Prov. 17:27;NCV).

Plan an occasional surprise "date night." He will love it.

"There are young figs on the fig trees, and the blossoms on the vines smell sweet. Get up, my darling; let's go away, my beautiful one" (Song of Sol. 2:13).

Keep intimate things private. Others don't need to know your every detail.

"He who covers a transgression seeks love, but he who repeats a matter separates intimate friends" (Prov. 17:9).

Plan a "do nothing — see no one" day once a month.

". . . Come away by yourselves, and we will go to a lonely place to get some rest" (Mark 6:31:NCV).

Smile far more than you frown.

"This is the day the Lord has made; I will rejoice and be glad in it" (Ps. 118:24).

Exercise control.
Keep a lid on your temper.

"Do not be eager in your heart to be angry, for anger resides in the bosom of fools" (Eccles. 7:9).

Pray together.

"Devote yourselves to prayer, keeping alert in it with an attitude of thanksgiving" (Col. 4:2).

Never say aloud everything that you feel.

"Like apples of gold in settings of silver is a word spoken in right circumstances" (Prov. 25:11).

Accept apologies.

"But He, being compassionate, forgave their iniquity, and did not destroy them; And often He restrained His anger, and did not arouse all His wrath" (Ps. 78:38).

Once something is forgiven, never mention it again.

". . . Just as the Lord forgave you, so also should you"
(Col. 3:13).

Love your husband's family. They will always be an important part of his life.

"Your people shall be my people, and your God my God"
(Ruth 1:16).

Let your husband decorate one room in the house just for him.

"So I saw that the best thing people can do is to enjoy their work" (Eccles. 3:22;NCV).

Love him even when he is unloveable.

"Put on a heart of compassion, kindness, humility, gentleness, and patience; bearing with one another"
(Col. 3:12).

Tell your husband how special he is.

"The words of a good person give life, like a fountain of water" (Prov. 10:11;NCV).

Lean on your husband. He likes to be strong.

"The glory of young men is their strength" (Prov. 20:29).

Greet your husband with the positives of the day. Save the negatives for later.

"Pleasant words are a honeycomb, sweet to the soul and healing to the bones" (Prov. 16:24).

Never be too busy for your husband.

"For not one of us lives for himself, and not one dies for himself" (Rom. 14:7).

Cherish quiet moments together.

". . . I may come and find refreshing rest in your company" (Rom. 15:32).

Always keep your bedroom fresh, neat, and inviting.

"The sweet smell of perfume and oils is pleasant"
(Prov. 27:9;NCV).

Be a sounding board for your husband.

"The mind of a person with understanding gets knowledge; the wise person listens to learn more" (Prov. 18:15;NCV).

Be an encourager, never a discourager.

"But encourage one another day after day" (Heb. 3:13).

Get over hurts quickly.

"Smart people are patient; they will be honored if they ignore insults" (Prov. 19:11;NCV).

Think forward, not backward.

"Do not say, 'Why is it that the former days were better than these?' " (Eccles. 7:10).

Listen to your husband with your heart.

"Wives, be subject to your own husbands, as to the Lord"
(Eph. 5:22).

Make bedtime a fun time.

"Kiss me with the kisses of your mouth, because your love is better than wine. The smell of your perfume is pleasant like expensive perfume"
(Song of Sol. 1:2-3;NCV).

You don't always have to prove you are right. It's okay to admit you are wrong.

"Be completely humble and gentle..."
(Eph. 4:2;NIV).

It takes time to learn to like the man you love.

"Love patiently accepts all things. It always trusts, always hopes, and always remains strong"
(1 Cor. 13:7;NCV).

Be a helper through the thick and the thin.

"Therefore encourage one another, and build up one another" (1 Thess. 5:11;NAS).

Learn to say "thank you" often. Your husband loves to hear these words.

"I have not stopped giving thanks to God for you. I always remember you in my prayers" (Eph. 1:16;NCV).

Be your husband's greatest sports fan. Many times he will stand alone, except for having you.

"An enemy might defeat one person, but two people together can defend themselves; a rope that is woven of three strings is hard to break" (Eccles. 4:12;NCV).

Teach your husband what makes you happy. He wants to know.

"The mind of a person with understanding gets knowledge; the wise person listens to learn more" (Prov. 18:15;NCV).

Your husband is yours and yours alone. Treat him as though he is the only one.

"Let marriage be held in honor among all"
(Heb. 13:4;NAS).

Comparing husbands is like comparing homes; everybody else's seems better, but very rarely is.

"It is better to see what you have than to want more. Wanting more is useless — like chasing the wind" (Eccles. 6:9;NCV).

Soothe your husband's hurts. He will adore you for it.

"A soothing tongue is a tree of life" (Prov. 15:4).

Attack the problem, not your husband.

"Speaking the truth in love, we will grow up in every way" (Eph. 4:15;NCV).

Remind yourself often of the blessings found in marriage.

"For this cause a man shall leave his father and mother, and shall cleave to his wife; and the two shall become one flesh" (Gen. 2:24;NAS).

Handle with care. Husband's hearts can be broken, too.

"Just as you want people to treat you, treat them in the same way" (Matt. 7:12;NAS).

Don't sulk.
You only hurt yourself.

"But now you also, put them all aside: anger, wrath, malice, slander, and abusive speech from your mouth"
(Col. 3:8;NAS).

PMS week is the wrong week to exercise your vocal chords. Practice Mostly Silence.

"Those who are careful about what they say keep themselves out of trouble" (Prov. 21:23;NCV).

Marriage is work, but work can bring extreme pleasure.

"The lazy will not get what they want, but those who work hard will" (Prov. 13:4;NCV).

Remember the peaks to help you through the valleys.

"Keep your eyes focused on what is right, and look straight ahead to what is good" (Prov. 4:25;NCV).

Learn how to handle frustration or frustration will handle you.

"With patience you can convince a ruler, and a gentle word can get through to the hard-headed"
(Prov. 25:15;NCV).

Never underestimate prayer.

"Pray in the spirit at all times with all kinds of prayers, asking for everything you need. To do this you must always be ready and never give up" (Eph. 6:18;NCV).

These Pearls of Wisdom are sure to help you get through the adjustments of that Notorious First Year together. Build on these Pearls and in the years to come you are sure to have a life of untold happiness together.

May God bless you to that end!